THE LITTLE BOOK OF

ARSENAL

SECOND EDITION

NICK CALLOW | NEIL MARTIN

First published by Carlton Books in 2002
Second edition 2010

A CIP catalogue record of this book is available from
the British Library.

ISBN 978-1-84732-680-5

Printed in China

INTRODUCTION

People say that footballers speak with their feet and that is certainly true of those who have played for Arsenal, but as these quotations show, they and many others connected with the club can utter one or two words worth listening to when necessary. For new fans and life-timers, here are some of the gems from the great and the good who have passed through the fabled Marble Halls of Highbury and those who have made a new Home of Football at the salubrious new surroundings in Ashburton Grove.

Whether you want to discover the real reason behind Charlie George lying down in the centre circle after scoring his Double winning goal in 1971, or who prided himself on scoring good own goals, this is the place to find out.

From literary giants to illustrious fans, from one club record-breaker to another – for them, and everyone devoted to the club, there is only one Arsenal.

66 I am going to make
this the greatest club
in the world. **99**

HERBERT CHAPMAN
sets the standards in 1925

" There are two kinds of visionary: those that dream of a whole new world, and those who dream of just one thing. Chapman's vision was of the greatest football team in the world. His genius was actually creating something close to that. **"**

BERNARD JOY

66 My aim is simple – to make Arsenal not just the best in the Premiership, but the biggest and best club in the world. **99**

ARSÈNE WENGER continues the theme some 70 years on

" The club is so superbly run. They say a swan serenely glides across the water and underneath it is paddling like mad. At Arsenal they don't even have to paddle, they just glide. "

MALCOLM 'SUPERMAC' MACDONALD

66 When you grow up with a club and you end up playing for them and winning things, you are from that club. I was produced here. I was formulated here. 99

LIAM BRADY

66 With a great name like ours only success is good enough. 99

DON HOWE now Youth Coach, continues to demand the best

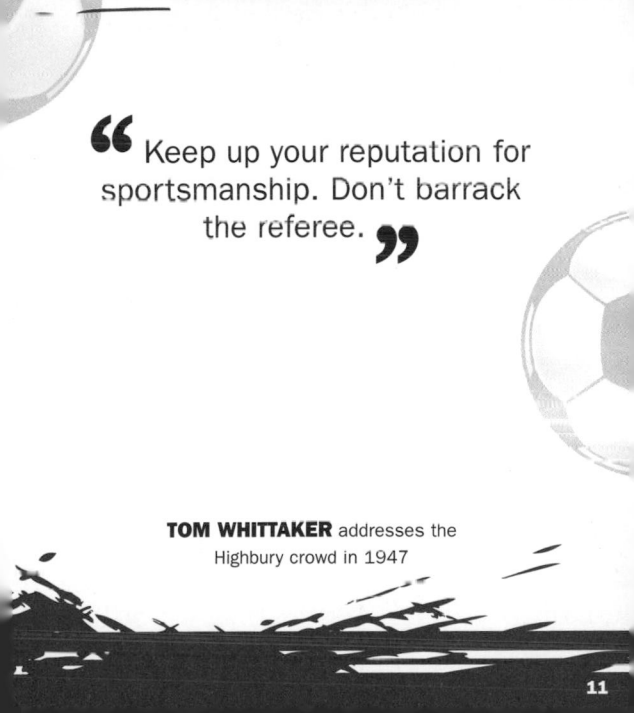

> **"** Keep up your reputation for sportsmanship. Don't barrack the referee. **"**

TOM WHITTAKER addresses the Highbury crowd in 1947

66 Herbert Chapman worked himself to death for the club and if it is to be my fate I am happy to accept it. **99**

TOM WHITTAKER as he takes over as manager

66 It works. I am just waiting until everybody has copied it, then I shall come up with something new. **99**

HERBERT CHAPMAN explains his famous 'M' formation

66 We are going for the Double. There is real character in this side and now we are going to show we can win League and Cup. **99**

FRANK MCLINTOCK after the semi-final replay v Stoke

> **"** I would not normally say this as a family man, but I am going to ask you for the sake of this football club, to put your family second for the next month. You have the chance to put your names in the record books for all time. **"**

BERTIE MEE to his players in run-in to the Double

> 66 Arsenal have got as much chance of being handed the title by Spurs as I have of being given the Crown Jewels. They are the last people we want winning the Championship. Now we mean to round off our season by beating Arsenal. 99

Tottenham captain **ALAN MULLERY** sets himself up for a fall in 1971

" There was no way we were going to be beaten. **"**

BERTIE MEE on the same game

> **"**I put everything into every game I played for Arsenal. As captain, I was motivating the side throughout every 90 minutes in front of 50,000-plus crowds every time we played.**"**

FRANK MCLINTOCK

66 My thoughts turned straight to the Cup Final and I was worried the crowd might injure our players. Some wanted their boots, which of course they had to wear on Saturday. **99**

DON HOWE plays down the celebrations – there was still the Cup to be won

66 People say why did I lie on the floor after the goal, they said I was tired. But I think I was a lot cleverer than people thought. 99

CHARLIE GEORGE reveals it was all a time-wasting plan after scoring the Double winning goal

66 My first football memory was Charlie George's goal to win the Double in 1971. After that game I decided to become an Arsenal fan. **99**

PAUL DAVIS

> **66** I was like an empty shell after giving everything on Monday night and was so whacked that it was almost as if it was someone else lifting the FA Cup. **99**

FRANK MCLINTOCK

66 They talk about Bobby Moore and Dave Mackay as great captains, but for my money McLintock is more inspiring than either of them. I am beginning to feel obsolete in the dressing room. 99

DON HOWE

" Above all we were blessed with a backbone of men with character who demanded excellence from others. **"**

DON HOWE in 1971

66 Winning the title against Spurs was obviously nice, but I just remember the Championship race being constant hard graft. And the FA Cup Final...was just a non-event as far as I was concerned... I can't say I particularly enjoyed that day. **99**

PETER SIMPSON shows you can't please everyone

66 The bloke who owned the Wimpy bar at Finsbury Park, where we all used to go on a Friday morning, said, 'I'll give fifty quid to anyone who gets a hat-trick.' And bosh, straight away – he was a bit sick. I didn't keep it all, Ian Ure made me split it. 99

JOHN RADFORD recalls a hat-trick in four minutes against Bolton in the FA Cup

" The first man in a tackle never gets hurt. **"**

WILF COPPING

66 When I am asked why I stayed so long the answer is simple, I never wanted to be anywhere else. I could have earned a lot more by moving, but that wouldn't compensate for all the good years with a great club. **99**

DAVID O'LEARY on what drove him to break George Armstrong's Arsenal appearance record

66 If I've got a good goalkeeper and a good stopper centre-half, all I need is the two best wingers and the best centre-forward there is. It doesn't matter what the rest are like. **99**

HERBERT CHAPMAN

> **"** When I first came to Arsenal I realised the back four were all university graduates in the art of defending. And as for Tony Adams, I consider him to be a professor of defence. **"**

ARSÈNE WENGER

" I made Tony Adams one of the youngest captains in Arsenal's history and I never had any doubts about him doing the job. The modern game is short of dominant personalities, so Tony stands out like a beacon. **"**

GEORGE GRAHAM

66 As far as I'm concerned, Tony [Adams] is like the Empire State Building. 99

IAN WRIGHT

" I play on the right, Tony on the left and we'll deal with whoever comes along, big or small. **"**

MARTIN KEOWN

66 He is a truly magnificent 'keeper. I am lucky to play in front of him every week. You look over your shoulder and feel safe. When I started playing for Arsenal I thought that if the ball went past me it would be a goal. I still go out with that attitude but with David behind me I know I don't have to sell myself. **99**

TONY ADAMS on David Seaman

" It doesn't really matter if it's a back four or a back five. The most important thing is that all of us have the same attitude to defending, which is an absolute determination to keep a clean sheet. **"**

MARTIN KEOWN

66 I think I lost my barnet [hair] flicking the ball on for all them years at the near post from Brian Marwood's corners. 99

STEVE BOULD on Arsenal's prolific corner routine

66 I've never been a goalscorer, only own goals. Good own goals. **99**

STEVE BOULD

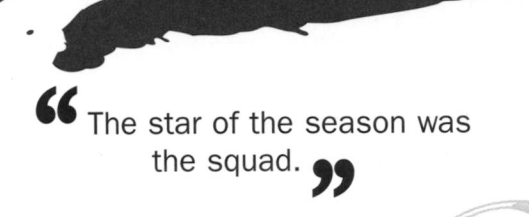

66 The star of the season was the squad. 99

ARSÈNE WENGER at the
end of 2001–02

66 There wasn't a lot of support, so I thought, 'Why not?' and next thing I knew it was in the back of the net. **99**

RAY PARLOUR explains his opening goal in the FA Cup Final 2002

66 The perfect end to a perfect campaign. **99**

Comment in the *DAILY MAIL* after Arsenal complete the Double on 8 May 2002

66 We love you Freddie because you've got red hair. We love you Freddie because you're everywhere. We love you Freddie 'cos you're Arsenal through and through. **99**

ARSENAL SUPPORTERS show their appreciation of Freddie Ljungberg's contribution to the 2001–2002 season

“ If you selected a team of nice people, Dave Rocastle would be captain. **”**

DAVID O'LEARY on the death of David Rocastle, March 2001

" George Graham was telling Lee Chapman that if footballers looked after themselves there was no reason they could not play until 35. Then he looked over to me and said, 'Well, maybe not you, Quinny.' **"**

NIALL QUINN recalls a much earlier conversation with his old Arsenal boss having broken the Republic of Ireland scoring record at the age of... 35!

66 I didn't score as many as I hoped, but it was nice that I always seemed to score against Tottenham. 99

CHARLIE NICHOLAS

66 In my time players had short hair, wore long shorts and played in hob-nail boots. Now they have long hair, short shorts and play in slippers. **99**

'GENTLEMAN' JACK CRAYSTON

66 The greatest one player over the years has to be Liam Brady. He is simply the best player I have ever seen in an Arsenal shirt. 99

TOM WATT, actor and radio presenter

66 It was a tragedy of monumental proportions for the club. 99

Manager **TERRY NEILL** after Liam Brady joins Juventus

> 66 There's a minute left on the clock, Brady for Arsenal...right across, Sunderland...It's there, I do not believe it, I swear I do not believe it! 99

PETER JONES commentates as Arsenal score the winner in the 1979 FA Cup Final against Man United

66 I think without a doubt that Dennis Bergkamp is the greatest player to have played for Arsenal in the last 30 years, for as long as I can remember. **99**

LIAM BRADY

Other clubs never came into my thoughts once I knew Arsenal wanted to sign me.

DENNIS BERGKAMP

66 If Ryan Giggs is worth £20 million, Bergkamp is worth £100 million. **99**

MARCO VAN BASTEN

66 I started clapping myself, until I realised that I was Sunderland's manager. **99**

PETER REID after Dennis Bergkamp scores

against Sunderland

66 I've trained against the likes of Dennis Bergkamp and that can make you quite nervous. **99**

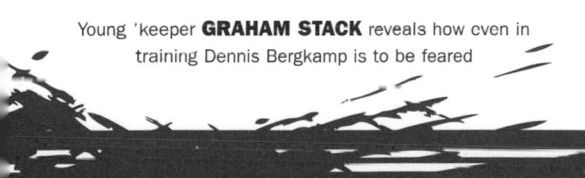

Young 'keeper **GRAHAM STACK** reveals how even in training Dennis Bergkamp is to be feared

" I saw John Jensen
score for Arsenal. **"**

FANS' T-SHIRT after John Jensen finally scores in his
98th game for the club

66 You can attack for too long. **99**

HERBERT CHAPMAN

66 Coupled with his sincerity and his loyalty to all his bosses, he had a trait few of us are blessed with – an ice-cold temperament. 99

TOM WHITTAKER on Cliff Bastin, previous holder of Arsenal's goal-scoring record

" The Third Division footballer may not be a soccer artist, but when it comes to the heavy tackle, he ranks with the best. **"**

CLIFF BASTIN following Walsall's shock 2–0 win over Arsenal in 1933

66 The centre-forward's drunk, Mr Allison. 99

TED DRAKE to manager George Allison after he had just downed a bottle of lemonade that was being used to highlight tactics

66 For you lad – and there's
no hard feelings. **99**

ASTON VILLA PLAYERS having signed the
match ball for Ted Drake after he had scored
seven goals against them in 1935

66 To be mentioned in the same breath as Ted Drake and Cliff Bastin is a great honour. 99

IAN WRIGHT becomes Arsenal's record goalscorer

" What's it like being in Bethlehem, the place where Christmas began?
I suppose it's like seeing Ian Wright at Arsenal. **"**

BRUCE RIOCH

" My image of the day will always be of the joy of the whole team when he broke the record. That shows how he is accepted by everyone. It was an historical moment. Maybe it will be 100 years before the record goes again. After all, it has stood for so long and Arsenal had some great strikers. **"**

ARSÈNE WENGER on Wright's goalscoring record

" The English players can do a lot for the French guys when they come. We can let them know what they're in for. **"**

LEE DIXON

66 We won the league at Old Trafford, we won the league in Manchester. **99**

ARSENAL SUPPORTERS reflect on the achievements of 2002

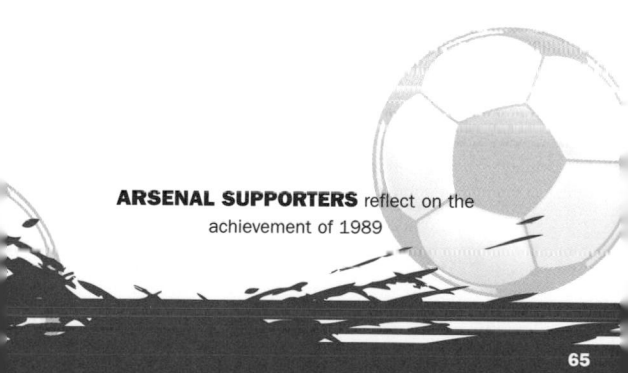

“ We won the league
on the Mersey, we won the league
on Merseyside. **”**

ARSENAL SUPPORTERS reflect on the
achievement of 1989

> **"** Good old Arsenal, we're proud to say that name, While we sing this song we'll win the game. **"**

ARSENAL SUPPORTERS

66 Christ, they've only lost one game. When was the last time that was done, a hundred years ago? **99**

SIR ALEX FERGUSON can hardly believe Arsenal won the League in 1991 losing only once

" Arsène who? "

TOM WILLIAMS, a lifelong supporter, reacts to Arsène Wenger's arrival on the back page of the *Daily Express*

❝ When he arrived, it was Arsène who? But I had seen this guy at close quarters. I had seen him work at Monaco, seen how he dealt with players and the public in general. **❞**

DAVID DEIN sets the fans straight

❝ He has given us
unbelievable belief. **❞**

PAUL MERSON on the impact of Arsène Wenger

66 I think in England you eat too much sugar and meat and not enough vegetables. It's silly to work hard the whole week and then spoil it by not preparing properly before the game. **99**

ARSÈNE WENGER gets out the broccoli and prepares to change the diets of Arsenal players forever, October 1996

" It is new to me to have someone checking your diet and giving you all kinds of tips – what to eat, when to eat, how to chew, when to eat chicken, when to eat fish, when to eat meat. You would think that is easy. "

GIOVANNI VAN BRONCKHORST

66 He is a hybrid. He is highly intelligent – he speaks five or six languages. He is cool, calm and collected, a great tactician. He also knows a lot about medicine. It's very rare that you find all that in a manager. **99**

DAVID DEIN continues to make his point about Arsène Wenger

> **Sometimes there is nothing better in life than being a Gooner.**

KEVIN CAMPBELL

66 Going to matches at Highbury is like visiting church, it's the stuff of sustenance for the community's infrastructure. I love it on matchdays when the whole area becomes a sea of red. It's a special thing. 99

DAVID SOUL aka Hutch, gets the Highbury bug

> **"** Tottenham tried to sign me but I held off and came to Arsenal because Arsène Wenger was here. **"**

EMMANUEL PETIT

> **Petit borrowed cash from Alan Sugar to take a cab to Highbury and sign for Arsenal.**

IT GETS EVEN BETTER – a newspaper headline on Petit's route to Highbury

" He took time to understand me, to understand my wild side. He worked on my psychology. He spent many hours talking to me and he understood what I could and could not do. When I think about what I could have become, I owe everything I am now down to Arsène. He is the greatest man I know. "

EMMANUEL PETIT gets some help from Arsène Wenger

" If a player doesn't like playing over winter and thinks there should be a winter break they shouldn't go to England. That's the way they play the game there and it's no secret that you have to play some tough games in tough conditions. **"**

MARC OVERMARS on foreign players moaning about playing in England

> **"** All Europe thought Overmars was dead because of his damaged knee. But in every important game we have had this season, he has scored. He has got great mental strength. He is a world-class player. **"**

ARSÈNE WENGER after the 1998 FA Cup Final

> **"** Seriously, I was the only player at Ajax who used to have fried eggs for breakfast everyday. It's one of my superstitions. If I don't have a fried breakfast in the morning, I won't play or train well. **"**

MARC OVERMARS' secret to scoring the Double-winning FA Cup Final goal in 1998

66 I get a shiver when I think about the Double every now and then, but my philosophy is simple. What is past is gone. What is important is what lies ahead. 99

1998 Double winning captain **TONY ADAMS**

66 There are more skilful right-backs, better tacklers, more accurate passers and certainly those with a better first-time control of the ball. But when it comes to concentration, commitment and maximising what you've got, then Lee takes some beating. **99**

GEORGE GRAHAM In his autobiography about Lee Dixon

" I am not worried about Premiership football, I came here fully aware that English football is very physical and full of tackling. It is a style of play that will suit me just fine. **"**

PATRICK VIEIRA sends out a warning on the day he signs for Arsenal

" Patrick Vieira is simply the king of midfield players in the English game. Not one player can get near him. **"**

MICHAEL THOMAS likes Patrick Vieira too

66 Robert Pires was quick to emphasise that he is not Marc Overmars, he is Robert Pires and we must not forget that. 99

LEE DIXON knows that Robert Pires is Robert Pires

❝ When I first heard the fans chanting, I thought they were booing me. But I soon understood what they were saying and that they like me. **❞**

KANU(uuuuuuuu)

" ARSENAL WIN THE WORLD CUP "

DAILY MIRROR headline salutes Arsenal's (France's) 1998 World Cup win

" That's what they teach you at Arsenal. You have to win, wherever you play – home or away, youth team, reserves or first team – you have to win a football match. **"**

PAUL MERSON

❝ Those that say it is the taking part and not the winning that is important are, for me, wrong. It is the other way round. **❞**

TONY ADAMS

66 I used to enjoy movies and going to the theatre, but I don't have much time for that now. My way of relaxing is to watch a football match on television at home. I suppose for most men that might cause trouble at home, but at least I have the excuse that it's my job! **99**

ARSÈNE WENGER

66 I love the crowd and the atmosphere that you can only get by being around a bunch of Londoners at Arsenal. **99**

ROGER DALTREY, of The WHO

" You can be feeling tired towards the end of a game, but the Arsenal crowd picks you up when they start cheering and that carries you through to the end. **"**

RAY PARLOUR on Arsenal's 12th man

66 Ray is without doubt the funniest player I've ever trained with. It's so important to have players such as Ray involved with the group, for his contribution on the field and spirit off it. I only wish I could understand more of what he says. **99**

GILLES GRIMANDI on Ray Parlour

66 To me, he will always be the Romford Pelé. **99**

Ray Parlour finds an admirer in **MARC OVERMARS**

66 I vividly remember a nil-nil with Leeds. It was one of my all-time favourite matches – only an Arsenal supporter could say that of a goalless draw. 99

RAY DAVIES of The Kinks

" It is not so enjoyable to score goals if the team does not win. "

FREDDIE LJUNGBERG

> **"** Ian Wright, Wright, Wright. So good, they named him thrice. **"**

JONATHAN PEARCE

66 It's a magnificent club and they really do look after the people that work for them, not just the players. **99**

KENNY SANSOM

66 I've made my decision and I just hope people respect it. I could have earned more money by going abroad, but I felt this was the place to be. **99**

SOL CAMPBELL on signing for Arsenal, 2001

66 I don't understand the reaction, it is only a game when all is said and done and Sol is such a lovely lad. **99**

PAT JENNINGS, who made the same move across North London

66 Before I came here, I would speak to the Manchester United players and they told me what it was like. Now I know what they were talking about. No one will roll over in games when you are with Arsenal, but I have adjusted now. I am ready. **99**

SOL CAMPBELL

" We have all had more fun than this. Have you ever known a colder night? **"**

MARTIN KEOWN after the defeat by Shakhtar Donetsk in Moscow, November 2000

66 Kenny Dalglish came on at the same time as me and everyone expected him to win it for Liverpool. But here I was, a ginger-haired nobody, setting up the winning goal for Arsenal. **99**

PERRY GROVES on the 1987 League Cup Final win over Liverpool

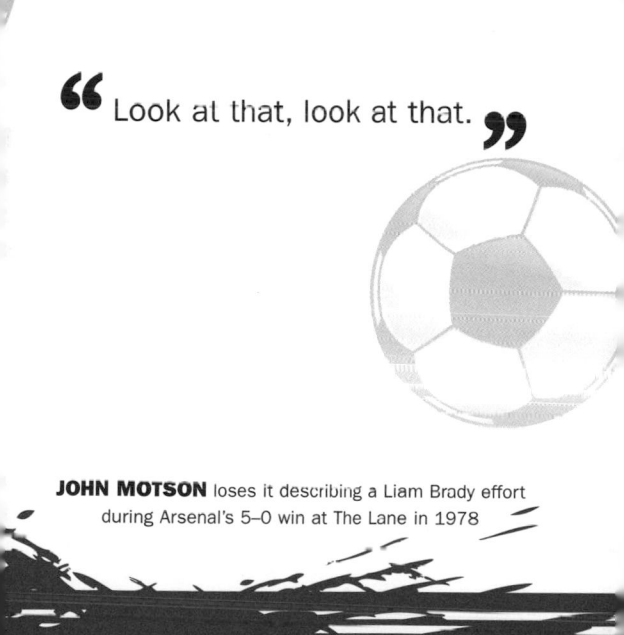

66 Look at that, look at that. **99**

JOHN MOTSON loses it describing a Liam Brady effort during Arsenal's 5–0 win at The Lane in 1978

> **"** I think they thought I had gone past my best, so I had to leave. **"**

PAT JENNINGS leaves Tottenham and still has four cup finals in him

**" A move like this only happens
once in a lifetime. "**

CLIVE ALLEN signs for Arsenal from QPR for £1 million and
leaves two months later, without playing a competitive game,
to go to Crystal Palace

66 I never thought of taking him off. It's nothing to worry about, it gives the face character. **99**

GEORGE GRAHAM after Andy Linighan, complete with broken nose, headed in the history-making winner in 1993 FA Cup Final replay

66 That will always be a memory for everyone else I suppose. The winner's medal and scoring the goal are my memories. **99**

STEVE MORROW reflects on being dropped by Tony Adams and breaking his collar bone after the 1993 League Cup Final replay

" You can practise penalties, but you can't recreate the pressure. I've taken a penalty against Man United in the Charity Shield and as I put the ball down I suddenly realised the goal looks as big as a matchbox. **"**

DAVID SEAMAN

66 Once we went a goal in front I knew we had a chance because our strength is keeping clean sheets. We had a team of heroes tonight and none more so than Alan Smith. **99**

GEORGE GRAHAM, after 1994 Cup Winners' Cup Final win over Parma

The tension I feel during a game is appalling. You would think it gets better as you get older, but it doesn't.

JOHN CHALLIS, aka Boycie of *Only Fools and Horses* is no plonker

"It's one–nil to the Arsenal. That's the way we like it.**"**

Some things never change – **GEORGE ALLISON**
in the film *The Arsenal Stadium Mystery*

> **"** I have not a single bad word to say for The Arsenal – it is a great club to play for. **"**

CHARLIE NICHOLAS

66 I was very very lucky to play for Arsenal and win all those trophies, but when people turned up for my testimonial in appreciation for what I had done for the club, it was very humbling. Very emotional, but it is every time I go back to Highbury, even as a spectator. **99**

PAUL MERSON

> **❝** I never had a proper chance to say farewell to the Arsenal fans. This will be a great opportunity to do it properly. **❞**

IAN WRIGHT before Lee Dixon's testimonial

66 It was very nice for me to play in Ian Wright's testimonial! The occasion surpassed all of my dreams. Every player likes to think he is appreciated and the fans tonight were simply magnificent. 99

LEE DIXON after Wrighty had stolen the limelight in his game against Real Madrid, November 1999

> **❝** I can't wait to put the boots back on and step out in the old red and white of my beloved Arsenal. **❞**

IAN WRIGHT's passion is still clear as he prepares for a Masters Tournament at the age of 37

> **"** We've had a lot of good times, but you don't know how good they are until you have the bad ones. **"**

TONY ADAMS

" It sounds ridiculous, but I always put my watch into the right pocket of my trousers. If anybody wants to nick it, they'll know where to look now I suppose. "

Superstitious **STEVE BOULD**

" I told my son Josh that Howard Wilkinson wanted Daddy to play for England. He told my daughter Olivia and they had tears in their eyes as they asked me, 'Does that mean you're not going to play for Arsenal any more?' "

LEE DIXON following a surprise England return

❝ Arsenal come streaming forward now in surely what will be their last attack…A good ball by Dixon, finding Smith…For Thomas charging through the midfield…Thomas…It's up for grabs now…Thomas…Right at the end…An unbelievable climax to the league season, well into injury time…The Liverpool players are down, abject…Aldridge is down,

Barnes is down, Dalglish just stands there, Nicol's on his knees, McMahon's on his knees…Suddenly it was Michael Thomas bursting through, the bounce fell his way, he clipped it wide of Grobbelaar and we have the most dramatic finish maybe in the history of the Football League. **99**

Commentary by **BRIAN MOORE**, 26 May 1989, as Michael Thomas scores to clinch the Championship, at Anfield

66 All that was on my mind was Bruce Grobbelaar. I didn't think about what rested on that one shot. 99

MICHAEL THOMAS, 1989

> **"** The football Arsenal play now is what you dream of playing. It's smooth and velvety. **"**

MICHAEL THOMAS – still a fan over ten years later

66 Kanu is feeling very down. He's very sad. It was an accident. We didn't want to cheat and Kanu didn't know what happened. He didn't understand at all because he's a very fair player. 99

ARSÈNE WENGER on the goal that never was against Sheffield United in the 1999 FA Cup

" It was a big mistake. They threw the ball for me and I was all on my own. I passed it and after that I don't know. I only realised something was wrong when the United players went up to the referee. I was not happy, they [Sheffield United] were not happy. **"**

KANU

" It is obviously an unprecedented situation but one we could not ignore. Everybody in football will welcome Wenger's sporting gesture and he should be congratulated for it. "

FA spokesman **STEVE DOUBLE** congratulates Arsenal on their offer to replay the game

> **Kanu is Kanu. He is the man. He has the ability to do special things and I love to watch him play.**

THIERRY HENRY

" I always like to score near the 'keeper. I like to do my tricks and when I see the 'keeper, I have to take him on. "

KANU

" I remember almost hitting the clock at Highbury and was ready to tell the manager that I wanted to go back on the wing, but I knew he believed in me and that was enough. **"**

THIERRY HENRY was not always confident in front of goal

66 Nicolas Anelka did a lot for this club, especially in the year we won the Double. Up front, he and Dennis Bergkamp were fantastic. He also had the big responsibility of taking over from Ian Wright. People who don't know him have the wrong image of him. He is a lovely guy off the pitch and a tremendous player on it. **99**

PATRICK VIEIRA

66 I would never play in England
in another shirt other
than Arsenal's. 99

PATRICK VIEIRA

66 When you see them keeping the manager, wanting to build a 60,000-seat ground, wanting to win things – that's the ambition I have...I believe in the chairman and the board. I believe they will put everything right to make Arsenal one of Europe's biggest clubs. **99**

PATRICK VIEIRA

" It was a surprise, but a very pleasant one. I had not planned to become a football club manager. **"**

Arsenal physio **BERTIE MEE** is appointed Arsenal manager

> **"** A wise, shrewd, hard little man...
> full of character and pride.
> No one's fool, a man-manager
> of top class. **"**

Chairman **DENIS HILL-WOOD** praises
Bertie Mee

" Only the players are important. I am not important. **"**

A modest **BERTIE MEE** at the time of the 1971 Double

" Everyone knows I'm an Arsenal supporter, I watch them all the time, and for someone like myself who grew up standing on the terraces and then jumped over and played with the players I actually idolised was just fantastic. **"**

CHARLIE GEORGE on fulfilling his boyhood dreams

He should get criticism. That is football. It makes the game exciting.

JENS LEHMANN, prepares for Ashley Cole's return

66 I supported Chelsea, but my Dad was a big Arsenal fan so I went to Arsenal and I owe my Dad a lot for that. 99

PAUL MERSON proves that sometimes you need a little pointer in the right direction

" I did not have a choice, but I am so glad I was born an Arsenal supporter. "

STUART BARNES, former England
rugby international

" If you lose hope, or lose belief, you may as well get out of football. **"**

GEORGE GRAHAM

" It was of course very special for me to be made skipper. Captaining this fantastic club is a great honour, no matter what the occasion. **"**

RAY PARLOUR on captaining the team in 2001

66 Part of the English game is that it's physical and enjoyable and... everybody I invite from a foreign country who watches the game says exactly the same: 'There's something special here...' **99**

ARSÈNE WENGER

66 Marriage usually stabilises. It gives players a natural discipline – they have to go home. **99**

ARSÈNE WENGER

I've not had to tell people like Robert Pires, Thierry Henry and Sylvain Wiltord about the FA Cup because they saw with their own eyes how much it meant when we played Tottenham in the semi-final at Old Trafford.

PATRICK VIEIRA

66 It was only 2–1, but the score does not reflect the total dominance we had over them. Even Spurs fans were saying afterwards that they couldn't believe it was only 2–1. **99**

Bob Wilson reflects on the 2001 FA Cup semi-final win

" The international game does nothing for me – it is the Gunners that turn me on. **"**

TV presenter **LISA ROGERS** shows her true colours

66 Second in the league might be good enough somewhere else, but not at Arsenal. **99**

MARTIN KEOWN

66 We nearly didn't sign him because the letters did not fit on his shirt. **99**

DAVID DEIN on the signing of Giovanni van Bronckhorst

> **"** I want to explode with Arsenal. There are trophies to win and unless there is a change of heart from the club, I want to win some. **"**

SYLVAIN WILTORD

" To be frank, when I first arrived I didn't think I would end my career here, but I am very happy. I am playing better than I have ever played and I have to thank English football for that. "

ROBERT PIRES

66 When I came to England I knew I had the ability, but mentally I wasn't strong enough. You see someone like Tony Adams before a game... He prepares for a match like a warrior. **99**

THIERRY HENRY

66 I enjoy my life in London. I love wearing the Arsenal shirt and I get a very special feeling every time I put it on. It is something in my heart and I hope it is something that will stay with me. The matter is not only in my hands because if I stop scoring goals maybe the club will not want me, but if I can still play, I would like to spend all my career here. **99**

THIERRY HENRY

> " We all want to be the best and I believe I can be the best with Arsenal. I have a long-term vision for the club. "

ARSÈNE WENGER

66 I thought football's greatest honour was to captain England. I was wrong. It was to captain Arsenal today. **99**

JOE MERCER addresses a banquet after Arsenal were defeated in the FA Cup Final by Newcastle in 1952

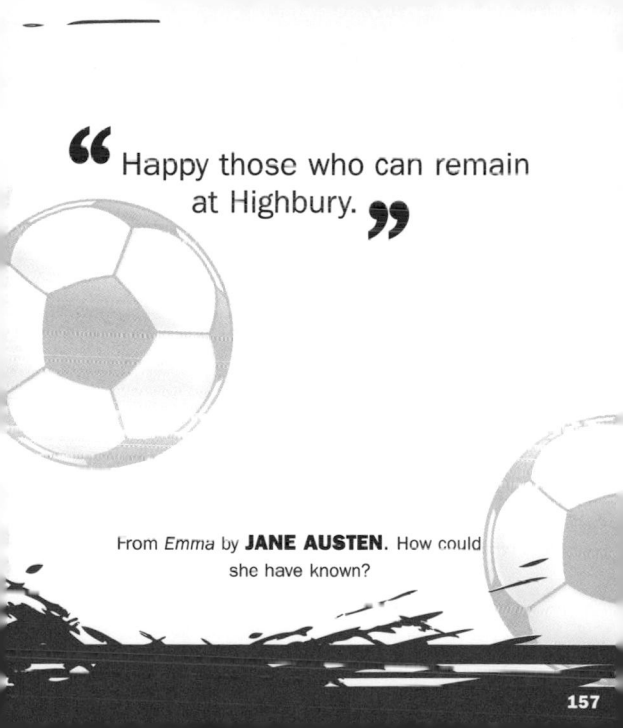

> **"** Happy those who can remain at Highbury. **"**

From *Emma* by **JANE AUSTEN**. How could she have known?

❝ I think it is very difficult to encapsulate in any succinct way what Arsène Wenger has done for this club. His discipline and his vision are why we are in a new stadium and why we are redefining the way the game can be played. He has created a young squad that has a tremendous future without having the resources that some other teams have. **❞**

Arsenal chief executive **IVAN GAZIDIS**, March 2010

66 I kissed the ground goodbye. Highbury is just a special place. **99**

THIERRY HENRY after his hat-trick farewell to the Home of Football secured a 4–2 win over Wigan, and Champions League football at Tottenham's expense, May 2006

" I have sympathy for Manchester United. They played very well and it is difficult to lose games like that when you have the chances. But that is part of the game. Out of 10 cup finals you win a few and lose a few and today they lost. They created more chances than us but they didn't take them. **"**

ARSÈNE WENGER reflects on the FA Cup Final penalty shoot-out win over Manchester United, May 2005

" I am really happy here and it is one of the best clubs I have ever seen. Everybody treats you like a king. I really appreciate it. I always wanted to play for a big club like Arsenal. **"**

CESC FABREGAS, February 2005

66 I think we can go a whole season unbeaten. 99

ARSÈNE WENGER makes an outrageous statement at the start of the 2002–03 season

66 Somebody threw me a T-shirt after the trophy was presented which read 'Comical Wenger says we can go the whole season unbeaten'. I was just a season too early! **99**

WENGER on an outrageous achievement of going an entire season unbeaten, May 2004

" It sticks in the craw because nobody likes The Arsenal, but you simply can't help but enjoy watching the football they play. **"**

BRIAN CLOUGH after seeing Arsenal equal his Nottingham Forest side's record of 42 games unbeaten, 2004

66 I just think it's something amazing, if you look at the number of goals we scored in these 43 games, and the number of victories we had, and the quality of our football, in modern football it is something amazing. **99**

ARSÈNE WENGER on breaking Nottingham Forest's unbeaten league record, August 2004

66 When you give success to stupid people, it makes them more stupid sometimes and not more intelligent. 99

WENGER responds to José Mourinho's claim that he was a voyeur, November 2005

66 When you represent a club it's about values and qualities, not about passports. **99**

WENGER on his side's lack of English players en route to the 2006 Champions League Final

It's like you wanting to marry Miss World and she doesn't want you. I can try to help you, but if she does not want to marry you what can I do?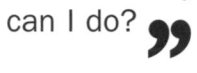

WENGER explains the on-off transfer of José Antonio Reyes to Real Madrid, 2006

66 He's like our dad in the team –
he is our dad. Every time when we
get a little bit down, he always calls
us to try and speak with us and
that's very important for us and I
am very, very happy to get him as
our manager. **99**

EMMANUEL EBOUÉ on Le Boss, post-match August 2009

66 I remember I took away the chocolate bars [on the way home] and the players were singing 'We want our chocolate back'. **99**

WENGER reflects on his first game in charge ahead of his 500th at the helm, August 2005

66 You do a lot of things in training for fun. It was not meant to be disrespectful to anyone, they just wanted to score the goal and finish the game. Robert came to me after the game, telling me he was sorry and that he had made a big mistake. As a manager, you have to live with these things. **99**

WENGER on THAT bizarre penalty miss against Manchester City when Pires tried to pass a penalty to Henry but failed dismally, October 2005

66 Barcelona can make other teams look ordinary but, I'm sorry, [on Wednesday] they looked really ordinary and especially considering we had ten men. But I think we showed against the best team in Europe that we can play good football, even with ten. **99**

THIERRY HENRY following the Champions League Final in Paris, May 2006

" After two big defeats it was a big test of our mental strength, character and togetherness. They have shown once again that when their backs are against the wall they can respond by playing fantastic football. We still have an unbeaten league run and the championship to go for and that is the biggest title. I can only guarantee one thing with this team, and that is they will give everything to win each game. I have big respect for this team. **"**

ARSÈNE WENGER after a famous 4–2 victory over Liverpool; Arsenal trailed 2–1 at half-time having just been dumped out of the FA and European Cups, April 2004

“ You ask 100 people, 99 will say it's very bad and the 100th will be Mark Hughes. **”**

WENGER on Mark Hughes's defence of Emmanuel Adebayor after the ex-Gunner stamped on former team-mate Robin van Persie's face, September 2009

66 Everyone thinks they have the prettiest wife at home. **99**

WENGER after Sir Alex Ferguson claimed his Manchester United side had been the best team in England despite Arsenal winning the Double in 2002

❝ Despite the global warming, England is still not warm enough for him. **❞**

WENGER on why José Antonio Reyes wanted to leave Arsenal and return to Spain, July 2007

" What would give me more pleasure than scoring four at Anfield? Winning the Premier League or scoring five at Old Trafford. After the Liverpool game my team-mates congratulated me and made a lot of jokes: 'We'll do everything for you tonight! Do you want anything? Just say and we'll bring it running. Can we clean your boots? Or carry your bag?' **"**

ANDREY ARSHAVIN after scoring four at Anfield, April 2009

❝ It sounds great to hear 'Thierry Henry, record goalscorer for Arsenal'. Wrighty was a great player and will always be a legend at Arsenal. To beat his record is tremendous. **❞**

THIERRY HENRY scores his 185th and 186th Arsenal goals in his 303rd appearance, in Prague, to become Arsenal's record goalscorer and beat Ian Wright's club record, October 2005

66 Arsenal will be in my blood as well as my heart. I will always, always, always remember you guys. I said I was going to be a Gunner for life and I did not lie because when you are a Gunner you will always be a Gunner. The club is in my heart and will remain in my heart forever. **99**

THIERRY HENRY on leaving Arsenal, June 2007

❝ Gérard is an open-minded and passionate man. I am the opposite: stubborn and stupid. But sometimes stupid behaviour makes you win. **❞**

WENGER on the difference between him and Gérard Houllier

" At the moment I'm just swallowing it all as part of the humiliation. That's something one has to take in. But I think – and this is aimed at my dear manager – one shouldn't humiliate players for too long. I'm an Arsenal player and I won't just fade away quietly. **"**

JENS LEHMANN on his reaction after being dropped for Manuel Almunia, October 2007

66 I feel I had a contribution to Arsenal's attacking style but there are so many other factors. I was part of the start and then the boss came, Patrick Vieira, Emmanuel Petit, Marc Overmars and then on to this team where they're basically all world-class players. Maybe 15 years ago they wouldn't have played for Arsenal, but they do now and I helped that. **99**

DENNIS BERGKAMP on his part in building 'The Invincibles'

" Champions continue to go when normal human beings stop and that is what we want to show. **"**

WENGER On what it takes to become champions, December 2009

" Every time you feel you have responded with style and quality and to the expectations of the people who come to the stadium, you're happy. You feel you have been a little bit of a help in pushing the club higher up to a different level. I try to have a positive influence on English football. **"**

WENGER on reaching 500 games in charge of Arsenal, August 2005

66 If I don't smile tonight I will never smile. **99**

ARSÈNE WENGER after 5-0 Champions League win over Porto, March 2010

66 It's great to be back and play in such a fantastic environment. I am going to give everything for every minute that I play. 99

SOL CAMPBELL reflects on his first game at the Emirates Stadium for Arsenal – a 5–0 win over Porto

" Even though we didn't win the game people will remember that we won the title at White Hart Lane. That was really important for the supporters. You don't win the title every day. It happened that it was at Tottenham and that's special, but we would have done it [celebrate on the pitch] everywhere. We know it's special for the fans so you can't just leave and go home. They deserved it. **"**

THIERRY HENRY explains why the post-match celebrations at Tottenham went on, and on, and on and on and on and on and on, 2004

> **One nil in the Bernabeu**

February 2006 and Arsenal are the first English club to win at Real Madrid, leading to another take on the terrace classic first sung by **ARSENAL SUPPORTERS** at half-time at Paris St Germain en route to the 1994 Cup-Winners' Cup Final

66 We worked very hard for each other, maybe some will say we did not deserve to win but our spirit was fantastic. **99**

PATRICK VIEIRA scored the 2005 FA Cup Final penalty shoot out winner with his last kick as an Arsenal player

" I am Gooner. "

ANDREY ARSHAVIN tells fans the good news after signing for the club

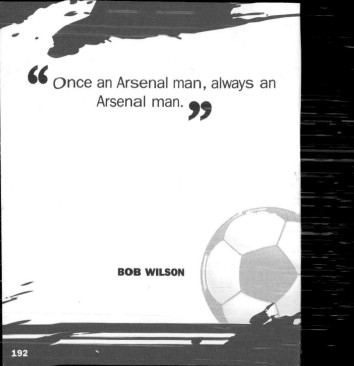

> **Once an Arsenal man, always an Arsenal man.**

BOB WILSON

" We do not buy superstars, we
make them. **"**

ARSÈNE WENGER